FIND THE POTENTIAL WITHIN YOURSELF

... it is a life changing book ...

Emmanuel Maudu

ISBN: 978 - 0 - 620 - 92469 - 6

Cover design by: Visible Content
Printed in the South Africa

CONTENTS

You are Talented

Show your Talent

Why Me?

Achieve, achieve and Achieve

Manage Yourself

Your worst Enemies (things you need to avoid)

Keep Learning

Excel what you do

Help others as well

Dedication

This is the dedication to all my readers. You inspired me to write this book. I hope you enjoy reading this book half as much as I enjoy writing it for you.

Preface

Find the potential within yourself; it's a life changing book. It 's a book made for people who are ready to change. Do not read this book if you 're not ready to change, read this book and you will be able to choose your direction. The book helps you to see the invisible part of your world. Everyone is talented, but people don't want to use their talent, they don't believe they have talent, but they believe others have talent and most people don't know that they are talented.

This book helps you to see the importance of your talent. By reading this book you're going to change, you 're going to start seeing things in a different way. You will develop a clear sense of your uniqueness and you will figure out how that translates in your work, career and life. It offers a practical and interactive approach to personal achievement.

It 's a personal resource book from which to draw ideas, strategies and practical techniques to help you find your talent. You're going to change, you 're not going to allow yourself sit down with that useful unique talent, which only need you to use it and change this world. You are going to use your talent, it doesn't matter what your talent is, try it -it works.

Chapte r 1

Change

You change for two reasons; is either you learned enough that you want to or you have been hurt enough that you have to. Change for the best is what everybody need, but not everyone is lucky enough, others experience down fall instead of rising. Changing for good need someone who is positive, who put an effort and always have a hope.

We are living in a world where things change every day, new ideas are being placed in a test and new invention are being made. The truth is people change too, it comes from inside; once someone start developing new interest, new passion and new feelings about anything, it is simply means the beginning of change in that person. Learning new things is in our nature, it helps to build us and shape our life. Everybody needs change in life; otherwise if nothing is changing, it's clearly means there won't be no improvement. It takes someone who's brave and have confident to say I want to change and be this kind of a person who is going to do this kind of a thing. The world need people who take charge, act and make things possible.

I like it when people talk about their New Year resolution; young people talking about their schools and dream careers, adults talking businesses, new jobs and dream homes. It encourages me to hear someone wishing to do or to have new good things. I truly respect and encourage others wish; when someone set a goal is capable changing something in this world.

7

Change is good; now take a step and be that person who is flexible enough to adapt to change. Open your eyes all the time and look around, learn, feed your mind with new information all the time and change to be someone useful in this world. You might be in sports, music, politics, science or writing like me; they all start from change, you must change your attitude towards what you want, it's the first step on your way to success. Life is a journey; we travel, along the way we meet different challenges, sometimes we go down and sometimes we go up. Challenges were meant for a human being, because we know and understand better, that is why we meet challenges most in our journey of life; the most important thing is how you respond to the challenge.

Understand Yourself

1. Who am I?

Most popular question, the one that you come across when you are having a conversation with yourself, in most cases most people tend to confront themselves like that when things are not going well in their life. Am talking about both young and old; and that is a very good question to ask yourself and how you respond to the question explain who you are. I remember back in high school; I also came across the popular question, and what do I really want in my life. It wasn't the simplest thing for me to answer by the time, I was still young and I didn't know that I am unique and special until one day, I was doing metric when I heard the school principal saying: "everyone is unique, special and everyone is talented on something. So in your life, you need to know and focus on what you want; that's if you want to see yourself going to tertiary you need to study and pass metric and then after you will see yourself going to tertiary". When I heard that from the school principal talking, I said to myself I am different. My answer gave me direction, I begun to see myself as a unique person, because I knew that I am not like other people, I am who I am. Everything that I do is different from what other people do. The way I think, the way I act, the way I do things, the way I react in different situations, the way I deal with my problems, the way I talk to other people and also the way I plan my future.

In your life the person that you need to know best is yourself more than anyone. From now on when you come across the popular question in your mind, know that you are different. You are who you think you are, because you are unique, the way you think and the way you do things is different from other people. The best way to understand.

9

yourself is to give yourself time to connect with yourself; I mean time to be with yourself, thinking about everything in your life. Is your own responsibility to find out what you like and want; same applies to what you don't like and what you don't want in your life.

2. Self image
"Self - Image is the key to human personality and human behaviour. Change the self-image and you change the personality and the behaviour." – Maxwell Maltz

Yourself image is the most important thing in life because everyone does things according to their self-image. Whatever you do you do it following yourself image, if you see yourself as a person who cannot drive a car, you can't drive it, but if you picture yourself driving a car one day, is going to be easy for you to learn to drive a car. You need to be careful of what you think of yourself because there are many people who gave themselves negative self-image and those who build positive self-image within themselves. It's simple to build negative self-image within you and it's also simple to build positive self-image either. By believing in yourself, you become what you want to be.

"Your work is to discover your work and then with all your heart to give yourself to it ." –Buddha

3. You are Talented
Maybe you already know or you don't know yet that you are talented; yes you are talented on something. Talent is any recurring pattern of thoughts, feeling or behaviour, which can be productively applied. Everyone is talented and unique. Thus if you're a Poet, singer, model, designer, writer, actor, artist, DJ, Athlete etc., this is what we call talent. Unfortunately most of us do not find time or make an effort to think and find out about what we're good at and work on it.

10

to perfect it. We're so busy getting through o ur day to day lives that there is no time for planning. We muddle from our day to day feeling that we're not getting anywhere, we often feel jealous of people who're succeeding and think, "if only I could be as lucky as Joe", only lucky really have very li ttle to do with it. It's funny how hard the successful people spend a lot of time practising what they do and after the luckier they get. Meaning that, success takes hard work. You need to work hard on what you do best in order to be a champion of what you do. Soccer star is a soccer star in the soccer ground, DJ is the best DJ in the studio, there is no other way that you can be a golf champion who doesn't play golf, you need to work hard playing golf and be a golf champion.

Find the potential within yourself, do something of your own, do not limit your actions in life; let the passion and thirst for success drive you. There is no need and time of undermining yourself. Draw a map and plan the direction of your life, where your talent and actions lead you, because if you don't care about where you're going, any direction will do.

Alice in wonderland   by Lewis Carroll

Alice- "would you tell me please which way I ought to go from here?"

The cat- "that depends a good deal on where you want to go" Alice- "I don't much care where..."

The cat- "Then it doesn't matter which way y ou go"

If you don't care about where you are going, there is no need for you to ask for a direction, you can only ask for a direction only if you know where you want to go. Choosing direction in your life is the only way which makes you to arrive were you are going.

11

My mother told me something one day that I cannot forget; her words sink right in my heart and they are always my mind. She said, "I always wanted to carry on wi th my studies after passing metric, I had a dream of being an accountant; but my mother had no money to take me further since my father passed away when we were still young. It was tough my mother was not working and life left me with no choice, but to forget about my dream and get married to your father. I was supposed to be working a better job than what I am doing now. So my son, am expecting something better from you; you are lucky your father and I we are here willing to help you all step of the way. You need to choose something that you like, something which is going to take you far and make us proud; it's all up to you my son, I believe in you ". I really feel for my mom, she failed to pursue her career and fulfil her dream because of her home situation. Her words motivates me than ever, she was not afraid of any challenge, she knew what she wants; she just didn't get privilege of doing what she was planning to do. That time things were tough, unlike now were people get scholarships, bursaries, and sponsors.

Most of us think of doing something everyday, but we don't do it because we're afraid, we don't believe in ourselves. We always ask ourselves, "what if I do it and it doesn't work, what are the people going to say?" that's fear of embarrassment which affects many people; it stops people from doing what they want to do. What I know is that we cannot escape fear; we can only transform it into a companion that accompanies us to our exciting adventure. Do something; take risk, one small or bold, and something that will make you feel great when yo u've done it. Go confidentially in the direction of your dream, act towards your dream, because you don't know what you can get away with until you try.

12

Your talent can make you be who you want to be, your talent can make you a hero, it can make people to respect you, it can make you rich, but only if you use it. You're talented and your talent is very important, if you use it, it can change something in this world.

Martin Luther King Jr, said "if a man hasn't discovered something that he will die for, he isn't fit enough fit to live", so, have you? Now is time for you to discover the nature of your own particular genius. Everyone is talented; everyone is a genius on something. Our talents are different, our uniqueness is our gift. No two people have the same qualities, vision and experience and our life's work emerges from our melting pot. You're who you are, you're incomparable. Nobody is like you and no one can share your talent with you; they can be like you but not you, because everyone is unique.

13

Chapte r 2

Show your Talent

"If one advances confidently in the direction of his dreams, and endeavours to live the life which he has imagined, he will meet with a success unexpected in common hours." –Henry David Thereau

Now is time for you to show your talent, a right time for you to act, make your dream come true. Don't be afraid of anything, is time for you for doing things you know best, something you're good at. But let me be honest with you, being successful doesn't happen by accident. It generally happens because the person has created and followed the overall plan. Like what my lecturer, Dr Kupa use to say some few days before we write his tests, "I wish you all good luck, go and prepare yourself. And remember try to be a little bit strict to yourself". Before his test he always wishes us good luck and he always remind us to read. He knew that if we have courage, we will prepare ourselves and pass his test. Those who like to ignore things, they always fail because they never go and prepare themselves.

Being successful need someone who is willing to work hard, someone who's dedicated, an ambitious someone with a vision, who's willing to act and change the world. I'm proud of my talent and that's why I'm using it. So what about you? Most of us have some very good talent, which only need to be put on practice. You're not wrong, what you think is better to be done. Be proud of your talent, do something about it, maybe it can bring change in this world.

14

When we're really honest with ourselves, we must admit our talent belongs to us, so it's how we use our talent that determines the ki nd of men we are; that's our duty. We all dream of happiness and successes, we all have ideas about what we'll do when we made it, we all feel as though we make difference and that our lives are important.

You can make any dream to come true, all you need is courage, have courage, you can do it, just believe in yourself. What I know is that everyone's task is unique, as his opportunity to implement it. You're unique and you've your own way of doing things that people will like.

Many people have already proved their talent in this world; some are still busy putting their talent into test out there; not only for themselves, but for their country as well, that's why we have doctors, artists, writers, actors, model, fashion designer, athletes etc. and now the question is; why not you?. Is time for you, be in a mission, have a vision and a goal to achieve. The first step in developing your mission is creating a vision of where you want to be in the future. A vision is a description of your ideal life or your personal definition of success. Planning on what you want to do is the only way which can make you successful one day. I'm saying this because planning is the activity which gets you from where you are now, to where you want to be in the future.

Those who are successful they achieve their success by aligning their uniqueness with their work or what they do. Love what you do, it's your talent, use it and enjoy. Don't be afraid of anything.

I was luck one day when I was sitting with my friend at the mall, waiting for an order at the restaurant, Willard Katsande, the well known Kaizer Chiefs player came and sat next to us, also waiting for his order. My friend said to him, "I was watching the awards ceremony when you win the best player.

15

of the season, congratulations, you are the best man; I'm your fan".

"Thank you", he replied. I asked him, "So what's your secret of becoming the best player of the season? " He smile and said, "Believing in myself and a lot of practice, am competing with my teammates and all soccer players around the world, I need to always be on top of my game ". He answered me and left me with no question, it was clear the way he put it; without any doubt he gave me the answer that I needed.

There are a lot of people in this world, who're afraid to be great. But they have talent which can make them to be great. They're afraid to be champions, only because they're afraid of the hard work they need to face and commitment required to be in the champion pantheon. But not you now, so go out there and be the champion. Be the best, it's who you are.

Be honest with yourself, you don 't have to pretend about anything. Decide today who you want to be. Finding a mission and then fulfilling it, is perhaps the most vital activities in which a person can engage. Abraham Maslow, put it this way, "if you plan on being anything less than what you are capable of being, you will probably be unhappy all days of your life".

Now you need to be armed with a vision, mission and a goal to achieve. You will be in position to take action and implement your strategies. You need to prepare yourself. What I know is that preparations pave the way. Now set your goal by looking at the following steps:

Steps of goal setting

Step 1: Objective- begin by clarifying your goal by asking yourself, what do I really want to achieve? Know what you want to do.

16

Step 2: Task- what is to be done. Ask yourself, what is it that needs to be done in order to achieve your goal.

Step 3: Method- how will it be done. You need to come up with some methods on how you're going to achieve your goal.

Step 4: Time required- how many hours a day or a week. Set yourself time, how you're going to use it. For example, if your goal is to become an athlete, you need to know how many hours you're going to practice a day or a week. Remember practice makes perfect.

Step 5: Target date- when does the job must be completed? You need to know the day you're going to complete your task. If it's a long term goal, don't worry; deal with it step by step. Know when to finish your first step of your goal.

Now you've set yourself a goal, you know what you're going to do. Start by taking one day at a time, then each day must become a step towards your goal. If the goal you want to achieve is a long term goal, don't worry. Carve big task into small bites and deal with only bite at a time. By completing one step of a difficult task, you encourage yourself to tackle the next step. It doesn't matter what your goal is...try it...its achievable!

Love what you do, act as if the world can see how your affairs are conducted. I believe in you, so believe in yourself, you can do it.

Just do good and laugh!

17

Chapter 3

Why Me?

"I think the purpose of life is to be useful, to be responsible, to be honourable, and to be compassionate. It is, after all, to matter: to count, to stand for something, to have made some difference that you lived at all." –Leo C. Rosten

You worth it, you have what it takes to be what you want to be. The world doesn't pay you for what you think or know, it pays you for what you do. So what about you? You want to get paid? Do something, nothing come easy.

People are constantly setting themselves goals and they achieve them. Those who don't do anything they see them as if they're different from them, they think maybe they were born like that, they think that they're not normal. You know what; they're normal, just like anybody. The only different is that they work hard to be what they wanted to be and they did it. They think of doing something and do it; th ey don't just think of doing something and leave it like that. By acting you become what you want to be.

In South Africa, we have people who've made their dreams come true, even when it was tough, they have done it! They are our hero, we love them.

I remember in the year 2002 when Mark Shuttleworth became the first African to go to the space; he proof to everyone that everything is possible. Sibusiso Vilane became the first black African to climb the world highest mountain, Mount Everest in 2003, things were not easy but he fights

18

until he become the first black guy to climb Mount Everest from Africa. Remember the world doesn't pay you for what you do think or know, it pays you for what you do. So do something, is not too late for you, it's your time .

Always look forward, look for the future, and don't worry about the past failings and mistakes; situation change. You can't live to the past; it's the future where you are going to spend the rest of your life. I have heard many people getting discouraged, one day I met three women in the train, and it was a Monday morning, they were all going to work. They were all complaining about the global recession, that prices are going up and their salaries are not enough to pay school fund, bills and groceries. They said, only business people are going to survive. We talked about starting a business. I told them that it's possible to start business in South Africa and it's possible to make it grow fast. But to do that, you need to be serious about it, you need to work hard. They were all looking at me like I was dreaming, one of them said; "you're still young, and you don't know how hard it's to look after a family". Another one said; "how can I do it, I'm old and I've a family to look after, you don't know how it's feels like to look after a family! It's very stressful, it's hard. I don't think I can manage to run a business. Now is no longer my time, I need to focus on my family. And even starting it, where am I going to get the money? You're still young; you will see it when you've a family"

I listened to what they were saying and I never ague with them, instead I asked myself, why people always talk about stress. What I know everyone get stressed sometimes, raising children doesn't mean that you should forget what you want in your life or try to do something new. Don't worry about stress; it can be the powerful force of success.

Don't forget that you're the only one who can make your dream to come true. People get paid for their hard work; they get paid for what they do.

19

Everyone in South Africa, remember the hard work of our first black president Nelson Mandela. He did a great job for everyone, things where tough for him, he spend 27 years in Roben Island. He came out of the prison and he didn't give up on his dream of becoming the South African president. It was a dream comes true for every South African, in 1994 when he became the first black president. We still remember what he did for us.

I know everyone want to be treated special, everyone want to get paid, everyone want to be remembered for the good things they have done and the only way to get all that is to work hard, use your talent. Don't be ashamed of your talent, because everyone has a unique talent and yours it's very useful. Work hard, someone is always watching.

In your life don't ever sell yourself short, you're smart enough and if you're competent people will have confidence in you. Choose your direction, most people choose to be average, but not you.

Those who are successful, because they enjoy what they do, they spend time practising in order to be perfect. You need to love what you do.

I was watching TV the other day, one of science documentary series; they interviewed different scientists, they talked about their inventions and future plans. I got amused and inspired by Elon Musk and Richard Branson interviews, was Elon Musk talking about his SpaceX project, a mission to go to our neighbouring planet Mars and start life there, working on making it a habitable planet. Richard Branson on the other side talking about his Virgin Galactic project were they are working on a place which will take people for a trip from here to the space and orbit for few hours and then come back. They talked about things that I never thought of it, you can tell they are enjoying what they are doing; I just said to myself that's history in the making.

20

You cannot work in a goal which you're not interested in, you won't enjoy and if you don't enjoy what you do, you cannot produce good results.

People are different, know yourself enough, and choose the Category which you think you fall under:

1. Those that make things happen

Those who believe that nothing is impossible, people with confidence. They believe in the beauty of their dreams. They think of doing something and do it. They are not afraid to take challenges and use their talent, they enjoy what they do. They believe in themselves. These are successful people, they make things happen. Most of them we know them, we love them, they're our heroes. But they just work hard. They don't follow money, money follow them.

2. Those who watch things happen

These are average people. People who doesn't believe in themselves, but they believe in other people. They don't think they can do something important, which other people can recognize. They doubt themselves, they don't believe in the beauty of their dreams. These are kind of people who have their own unique talent, but they are afraid to use them. Most of these people know everything which others are doing; they are always updated in everything. Why always watching? And not doing something.

3. Those who wondered what happened

Those who are lazy to think, they don't want to think about anything in this world. They are defeated; they are living in a different world, with nothing. They think they cannot be creative enough, to come up with something. Most of this

21

people, they are always criticizing other people. They don't see good thing which others are doing. They are not ambitious; they don't think they deserve something in this world. If your ambitions are dead, you better be buried. What are you living for?

22

Chapter 4

Achieve, achieve and Achieve

"The greatest use of life is to spend it for something that will outlast it." – William James

From where I am sitting right now I say; Achieve, Achieve and Achieve, because what you're doing is achievable. Yes, there is no need for you to doubt, and remember a goal or objective achieved is a success. Achieving is like travelling; before you start on a journey you must know your destination. I'm saying this because before you arrive, you need to travel knowing your direction, because if you don't, you might get lost along the way. You must plan your journey and predict difficulties and challenges, which you might face along the way. You need to open your eyes to the world around you. See everything in as much details as you can and ideally in a new way. If you have special interest in something, research it as thoroughly as you can. You can never know too much and know what; no piece of knowledge is ever totally irrelevant.

Achievement does not necessarily favour those with financial means or external support, but rather those with access to inner resources such as self belief, determination and creative thinking. Henry ford said, "thinking always ahead, thinking always of trying to do more, bring a state of mind in which nothing seems impossible". Make better use of your time; treat difficulties as creative challenges rather than as burdens to avoid. Just work hard and achieve everything that you want in your life.

23

1. Attitude about Yourself

This is all about yourself and not other people. When doing what you do, you need to have a good attitude about yourself. You need to feel good about what you are doing, you need to be proud and be confident about it. One of the reasons why people do not follow their mission is because of lack of self-esteem. Most people dreamed of doing something and wish to achieve it according to their plan, but because of lack of self-esteem, they fail what they wish to achieve only because they do not believe that they can achieve what they love.

In this world many people are unhappy in their career and are working at unsuitable jobs, because they are trying to fulfil someone else's dream instead of their own. Let me be honest with you, your success does not depend on the perspective that others have for you, it depend on what you do for yourself.

You must put aside the mentality that you are a victim of circumstances and that everything good is outside of you. In order to achieve your dream, you must believe that you are fundamentally good and whatever you want to do, you can do it. Abraham Maslow called the urge to maximize our individual talents, the desire for self actualization. He said that, "each of us desires to become everything that one is capable of becoming, what a man can be, he must be". You are complete and whole and you are continually growing. Know that your power comes from you and not someone else. You must think of the alternative and always aim high, believe in yourself, because if you don't, who will.

2. Attitude about success

"If you do what you have always done, you will always be what you have always been" - Unknown

The first advice that I can give you is that, be the actor rather than the acted upon. If you want to be successful, you must have a positive perspective and feel more in control of your life. Feeling more in control a person become an actor and not an acted upon. The actor move towards the goal, expecting to achieve it; everyone have a goal. Our goals direct our actions and our actions take us towards our goals and achieving our goals makes us successful.

Wherever we are, we are here because our goals and action led us here. You may sincerely want to achieve your goal, to be happy and successful, but deep inside your subconscious may think otherwise. You may have a hidden attitude that success will bring bad things, a deep belief that you are not deserving and perspective that there is not enough to go around. This attitude may subconsciously prevent you from being successful. To you success may be too over whelming or it might seem like too much responsibility. Jerry Gillies said, "the strongest single factor in prosperity consciousness is self-esteem; believing that you can do it, believing that you deserve it and believing that you will get it". I also agree with him, yes, if you do not have a good attitude about success, you can't be successful, if you don't believe that you can achieve something you will fail to achieve it because you don't believe in yourself.

Now I want you to recall that when you created your vision earlier in this book by setting your goal, you develop your definition of success. So now you are armed and ready, you are going to be a successful worrier who cannot afford to lose a battle; you are going to be a serial achiever.

25

You must believe that you are going to bring change around you, if not around the world. When you do something which helps others as well, it brings happiness in you and it can makes you more successful than you ever expected. What you should do is to identify your negative attitude and replace them with more appropriate one.

The world is full of opportunities, you have the power to fulfil your dream, because you are talented and one thing for sure, and you deserve to be successful. You need to believe that a goal can be accomplished and that you can accomplish it. If you can conceive of an action plan to achieve a goal, you have one step accomplished.

Chapter 5

Manage Yourself

"To understand oneself, to see oneself, to feel oneself, to own oneself....is to be oneself" - unknown

St. Francis de Sales said, "Have patience with all t hings, but first with yourself". Nobody knows you than your own self and nobody understand you than yourself. You are in charge of everything in your life; you are a leader, a director, an advisor and a guider of your own life. When you are doing what you do, using your talent, there are many things that you need to be careful of in order to be what you want to be. You need to be strong, learn to deal with many situations, because there are many challenges in life which makes people to lose focus in what they do. Always be yourself and keep on doing more. You need to understand and learn to deal with, pressure, lack of planning and lack of concentration.

1. Thrive under pressure

Pressure takes many forms and there are many causes of pressure, it may be generated by other people or situations or it may be self imposed. It can occur when you are working on deadlines, competition or having to perform different roles, such as parent; partner, son or daughter, friend etc. all at the same time or having to cope with the setback of change. You need to be careful and learn to deal with pressure because it makes people to lose focus or to give up on their dreams. It also causes many people not to cope in life. It causes stress, loss of temper, causes less effectiveness, makes people to lose focus, it causes restless, lack of concentration and it also creates bad moods in people.

27

"Worrying about a situation does not improve things; it's just a waste of a valuable time and energy"

-unknown

You need to understand that sometimes pressure can be the motivating force; it can bring up the best in people. When pressure is well managed, it can spur you on to greater achievement, whereas an inability to handle pressure can result in adverse reactions, including increase vulnerability to stress. What I know about pressure is that, it stimulates the body and mind, producing a variety of advantageous effects. So a wise man is he who learns what causes pressure and how to deal with it, because being able to deal with it helps people to realize how resourceful they can be. The more experience of thriving under pressure you have, the more confident and authoritative you will become.

3. Understand pressure

Accept that pressure is a fact of modern life and that everybody faces pressure in his/her journey of life, so it's important to learn how you can thrive under it.

To make pressure work for you, you need to reassess the way you react to it and learn coping strategies.

Coping strategies:

*Have smile in your face- Being under pressure or stressed, it doesn't mean that you should show it to everyone. You need to smile with people and they will smile back to you. By smiling you feel comfortable around people, you feel happy and you will be able to cope.

*Just feel more attractive- Is your responsibility to bath and wear clean nice clothes before you can live your house. Make sure that you look attractive and you will receive compliment from other people. You will be able cope around other people.

28

*Have sense of achievement- Just believe in yourself, you need to have that feeling of achieving in your heart. You need to stop worrying about the situation and focus on what you have to do.

*Have more energy- You don't have to get discouraged and feel lazy about the situation. You need to have that energy of working to achieve.

*Have faith in your ability- You know yourself, you know that you have the ability to achieve anything. You need to forget pressure, believe in yourself and work hard to achieve what you do.

2. Manage your time

"It's not the hours you put in - it's what you put in the hours"

-unknown

One of the biggest traps in today's life is the busy culture; the major problem with this culture is the habit of busyness. It gives rise to a "start early, finish late". The only problem with this culture is that it causes pressure, stress, restlessness and even headache. You need to avoid keeping yourself busy out of a sense of habit, duty or guilt, because all these factors reduce effectiveness and motivation. Think about how you could be less busy and be more effective, how you could work smarter and not harder.

You need to prioritise tasks according to their importance and not their urgency, so that you can always stay focus. More work load can make you lose focus on what you are doing. You need to realize that if you are always busy, you may not work effectively. Avoid working long hours to meet deadlines, learn to manage your time and avoid falling into an activity trap.

29

*Prioritising time

"Time wasted is never regained"

-proverb

You don't have to waste your time working on one task. When working on your goal you need to know when to finish your task and when to start with another task, one step at a time towards your goal. Avoid working on both tasks at the same time, because you won't be able to manage your time carefully. Never waste your time, know that time waits for no man.

Set deadlines for yourself

Know how many hours you need to work a day

Know how many days you need to spend working on a task **3. Building Self Assurance**

"Make it your goal to talk to new people wherever you go"

-unknown

Good influential look, sound and act convincing. All you need to do is to take steps to increase your confidence, improve your ability to emphasize with others and build trusting relationship. People will place greater trust in your ideas if you communicate with confidence. You should learn how to increase your poise and self assurance, make it your goal to talk to new people wherever you go. You also need to develop the ability to recover quickly from your mistakes and learning from your mistakes as well.

"If you focus on your imperfections when you look at the mirror, you will only harm your self-esteem. Accept your faults but recognise good points too"

-unknown

When you are building on yourself assurance, you must tolerate nervousness as the price you pay for progress. You don't have to worry by being nervous about anything you do, know that skills need to be practised before they can improve further. You must learn to stay calm in whatever situations, give yourself time to listen to other people carefully, ask questions if you don't understand and you also need to have confident when talking to other people. If you make mistakes, see them as learning opportunities; don't ever feel useless by making mistakes.

Ways of building yourself assurance:

*Organised- you need to be always organised, plan everything before you can talk or meet with other people. Make it your goal to always look and sound organised.

*Friendly- always has a smile in your face. You need to put people at their ease with some well chosen words and compliments. Talk to new people wherever you go.

*Energetic- always be decisive when you outline your ideas to other people. You need to look and sound confident in front of other people.

*Ambitious- always look for new opportunities; always try something new in your life. Don't be afraid to lead meetings and making presentations.

*Knowledgeable- you need to take everything seriously, don't be ignorant, try to know a little bit of everything in your life. Keep up with current affairs and organisational matters.

*Analytical- think through your ideas from angle and consider every objection. You need to become an optimist, look for solutions rather than dwelling on problems.

31

Cha pter 6

Your worst Enemies (things you need to avoid)

There are things that you need to avoid in order to get things done. You need to be careful and learn to deal with: Procrastination, lack of planning and lack of concentration.

1. Procrastination (to put off doing something)

This is the element of postponement, to put off doing something. It's the biggest time waster, which makes most people not to finish or delaying what they are doing. This is the habit which you need to avoid when you are working on your goal in order for you to achieve it. There are many things which cause procrastination or postponement, which you have to deal with in order to get things done: Stress; Lack of interest; Fear of failure, Problems; Special interest on something else; Relationship matters etc. Those who are successful they concentrate on what they do, they make sure they finish their task.

I have seen many people keep on postponing doing what they have to do and end up failing or giving up. You need to be careful and learn to deal with procrastination, because procrastination can cause you to fail when working to achieve your goal. Look at the following causes of procrastination and learn to deal with it.

Anxiety about the possible consequences of your action (troubled feeling in the mind caused by fear) - lack of confidence causes this. Those who have less confidence, they find it difficult to work on their task, because they have fear in their mind- fear to fail, fear to make mistakes, fear of what

32

others going to say about it. So they keep on postponing because they doubt themselves, don't believe they worth it and that they have got what it takes to achieve what they want in life. The only way to deal with this is to be confident about what you are doing, be proud of it and tell yourself that you are the only one who needs to work hard and achieve your goal.

Uncertainty over how to go about a task (not being sure about how to do what you have to do) - this is caused by not being sure about what to do when working on your task. Stop avoiding what you have to do because you are not sure about what to do or how to do it. Stop wasting your time by doing nothing, the only way is to start making a research and understand what you have to do. Then after understanding what you have to do, it's going to be simple for you to start tackling your first task. What I know is that, the task you have been avoiding, turn out less fearsome than expected.

2. Lack of planning

"Planning is the activity which get you from where you are now, to where you want to be in the future"- myself

Nothing good or major was ever been achieved without being planned first. There is no other way in which a person can achieve something which is not planned. In order to achieve something, you need to plan it first by setting your goal and planning every step which you have to go through working, in order to achieve your goal. Every successful people plan their things first in order to achieve what they do. I am saying this because there is no other way in which you can start a business and run it and end up being successful without planning everything. In everything you do you need to plan first, what I know is that, planning is the activity which get you from where you are now, to where you want to be in the future. A journey of thousand miles starts with a

33

single step. Is either you plan your journey, start it and arrive well or start a journey without planning first and fail or get lost along the way.

Lack of planning causes a lot of stress, causes people to give up on what they are doing, causes people to postpone their task, and it causes failure, because an unplanned task is the most difficult one. I have seen many people failing what they do, because of failing to plan.

The only way to get what you want is to plan how to get it first and do what you have to do in order to get it and get it at the end. Those who believe in doom and gloom they don't plan anything to get anything, they just wish or believe that they will get what they want without planning how to get it and do what is suppose to be done in order to get it.

While working on your goal, using your talent, you need to plan first before you can start doing anything, so that you don't have struggle and fail to achieve your goal. By planning you find it simple and far more enjoyable to work on your everyday task, because you will know what you have to do for that day.

There are following steps of planning which you have to follow in order to get things done.

*Time scale- you need to set yourself time before you can start working on your task. You need to know how much time is needed for you to finish the task.

*Deciding what resources is needed- you need to know, list and get all the resources which are needed for the task. Everything which is needed for the task must be well prepared before you can start working on you task, because you don't have to struggle about anything while busy working on your task.

34

*Breaking long term into small tasks - if the goal you want to achieve is a long term goal, don't worry, all you have to do is to break that goal into small attackable tasks. You need to know when to deal with the entire tasks one step at a time.

3. Lack of concentration

Being unable to concentrate on what you are doing is like failing to do what you have to do. Lack of concentration is one of the most dangerous things which cause people to fail achieving their goal. There is no other way that you can complete any task, without concentrating on it. There are many things which cause lack of concentration; things that you need to avoid in order staying focus on what you do. You need to learn to re-late to many situations. Lack of concentration causes postponement, decreases confidence, looses interest on something, causes less effectiveness and it also causes failure.

I remember the time when I was writing my final exam during my second year at the university, things where bad for me. I was dating a beautiful girl at the campus, and then I had rumours from some of my friends that she's been seen with another guy. I was really shocked to hear that, because I was really in love with her, I asked her myself and she said that it's a lie and that she only loves me. I investigated the story myself; the result convinced me that it was true; yes she was involved with him. I was a heartbroken man, I lost concentration in my studies and I spend most of my time thinking about her and what she did to me, because I trusted her and didn't want to lose her. I was doing four courses and I was supposed to pass all my courses, because courses were very expensive for my family and I knew that my parents were going to worry if I fail. At the end of the year when my results came back, I found out that I have failed one course; I was very disappointed because I knew that I had lost concentration in my studies because of her. My parents were

35

also disappointed because of my performance.

If you want to achieve your goal, lack of concentration is something that you need to avoid. Don't allow any thing to destruct you. By learning to deal with stress, problems etc., you can be able to concentrate in your task. Just concentrate and the world is yours.

36

Chapter 7

Keep Learning

"Learning happens in many different ways and learning how to learn is closely related to self-leadership"

-unknown

Many people believe that thinking is the most important way of knowing about the world. And I said no, because learning is the most important way of knowing about the world. Is the process which happens every day and it also happens in many unlimited different ways. There is no limit for learning, it doesn't matter your age, you are always learning any time and anywhere. When you die that's when you stop learning.

Learning happens when we move from thinking about what happened, to what tends to happen, this allow us to apply what we have learned from our experience to many new situations. Learning is highly meaningful for a number of reasons; because is rewarding, it gives more autonomy, it also gives power or means of self expressions, it also helps us model someone who is important to us and live like them, it gives us direction for the future and it's also interesting, because we are curious and we just want to learn and know what's happening around the world.

37

1. Always be curious

"Be curious always! For knowledge, will not acquire you, you must acquire it"

-unknown

Let your mind move on to something you want to understand more about, go on and find out, by asking question to the right people who can help you find what you want. You need to adopt a curious state of mind that enjoys the challenges of discovery. Discovering new things is a good thing, that's the way of knowing things in this world.

Never be afraid to ask, when people know what you are asking about, it becomes easier for them to give you the information that you need. In your life never ever feel stupid by asking, a wise man is he who always want to know than he who claim to know everything.

If you find yourself in a situation where you are afraid to ask about things that you want to know or situation where you are afraid to ask for something that you want; you need to ask yourself these questions:

What am I going to lose by asking?

Where am I going to get what I need? And

How am I going to get it without asking?

You need to answer yourself, and if the answer you have got it doesn't make you find what you want, is either the information about something or something you are asking for, then what I think you should do is to get rid of that fear, is not helping you with anything. You need to be confident and have a smile in your face, ask questions because you want to know.

38

"A person's mind stretched by a new knowledge never goes back to its original dimensions"

-Oliver Wendell Holmes

Curiosity is the best and simplest way of learning, all you need to do, is to ask couple of questions about the thing you want to understand, without feeling stupid or somehow and without telling yourself that you must have all the answers now or at the same time. You will see, all the things that you need to know will come to you much more easily, when you are relaxed.

2. Learning from experience (failure & mistakes) "Experience is

the best teacher"

- Proverb

Failure, painful though it may be, but it can in fact teach you something in your life. By finding out what went wrong and think of what could be done differently next time, you can turn failure into learning opportunity.

"You always pass failure on your way to success"

- Mickey Rooney

Whenever you make a mistake or get knocked down by life, don't look back at it too long. Mistakes are life's way of teaching you, everybody fails, no one taste a true success by living a very safe, uneventful existence, failure must be experienced along the way, but what is important is the way you handle failure. The problem with failing is that, most people take it personally and feel stupid about it. As a human being you need to know that you are a learning creature by nature and design, so you don't have to give up from doing what you do only because you have failed.

39

Larry Wilson said, "If we never make mistakes, if we never look foolish, if we never take a risk, we will never grow and we will never experience the exhilaration that exists on the other side of those fears. We became self limiting". You need to understand that failing is part of learning, you should learn from failing, when you look at mistake as a teacher, you enhance your own sense of self. I have seen it, most people feel stupid after failing, and they take it personal. Don't ever take failure personal; see it as a chance to improve, because in your life some of the greatest experience probably came from mistakes you made.

John Powell, put it this way, " the only mistake is one from which we learn nothing " and I agree with him. I have learn the tough way the year that I was repeating a course, the NSFAS money was not enough to pay for my room after covering most of my courses, which I had to pay for my other courses with my money; I had two options, paying for a room with my own money, which was very expensive or go and stay in a cheaper room off campus, which was boring. Then I decide to ask one of my friends who were staying alone in a single room if I can stay with him, and then I will pay him every month. He agreed and we stayed together nicely, we helped each other with everything in the house; we use to go partying and drink together, it was fun. I paid him well first and second months, the third month it happens that he had some financial problems; I didn't mind buying things we use to buy to pamper ourselves and also alcohol for us to go partying all weekends of the month. Things change when he ask me about the monthly rental money that we agreed on, it felt like a joke to me, he saw me spending money with him and he enjoyed too. By that time I had no money at all, I tried to explain to him that I don't have money and that the money I spent with him. He agreed everything, then he told me that I was supposed to give him his money first; that's when I realize that I made a big mistake, because he was right. He asked me to leave his room; I left and ask my other friend if I

40

can sleep in his room for couple of days before I get my own room off campus. He agreed but it was terrible because all of our friends use to spend time in that room playing some video games, including the one who chased me from his room. I was a laughing joke for all those days that I was staying there, sometimes I use to just go and spend time at the computer library just surfing internet until late to avoid being bullied.

I have learned a lot from that mistake, it was a lifetime lesson which is helping me today and still going to help me in the future. From that time I begin to know that agreement is very important, it has rules and consequences; you fail to deliver what you have promised, you face some consequences.

3. Learning from Rejection

Being rejected its very painful and on the other hand is a very good lesson, which is why almost every successful people face rejection along their way to success. In your life, don't ever take rejection as a problem; take it as just a lesson. Everyone face rejection at some stage of his/her journey. The only way is to accept rejection as just a lesson. You need to be proud that you tried doing something and get rejected; you didn't fail, because you still have more time to go and improve what you are doing. Rejection can happen because others do not recognise the value of what you are doing, but it doesn't mean that what you are doing is not important. If you are trying to do something and you get rejected at some point, do not panic because they are giving you chance to rectify where you got it wrong.

I used to take rejection as a big failure, but now I know that after being rejected, you still have chance to go and improve yourself, a time to go and rectify your mistakes. I have seen it when my friend Ronny got rejected at the

41

university because of his conditional exemption. He wanted to register for LLB Degree and they said he doesn 't qualify to do LLB Degree because of his symbols. I remember the time when he came to me asking for advice, he said 'what do you think I should do here, LLB is the only degree that I want, and I don't want to find myself doing something which I don't like'. When I answered him I said, Ronny I think you still have a chance for doing LLB Degree. How; when he ask. 'You can still go and improve your symbol at the college and next year that's when you can be able to come and register for LLB here at the university '. W hen I told him that, he starts to see it that it can work and he took my advice. The following year Ronny managed to register for LLB degree, he completed his degree within a record time and now he is working as a lawyer and the last time I had a chat with him, he told me that he's planning to open his law firm any -time soon.

Being rejected is painful and people take it serious and end up giving up on what they want to do. If you are doing something, using your talent, you need to know that you can be wrong sometimes and get reje cted, but that doesn't mean you are a failure, what matters is that you are trying to do something and you need to see that they are giving you chance to go and correct were you need to. You need to learn to accept rejection as another piece of feedback, another piece of data. Learning to deal with rejection is a critical part of a creative process.

4. Learning from others (role model)

In life we always dress like others, we always walk like others, we always talk like others, we always live like others and we always wish to be like others. That happens when you look around, and be able to select what 's good then leave the bad alone. It is always good to like good things which others are doing, and learning how they do it always helps us to

42

come up with the best way of doing our own.

I like the way how scientists carry on with the theories of other ancient scientists to achieve their goals; it is how most scientists are getting it done. Elon Musk name the car company Tesla after the inventor because it uses AC induction motors, which is an architecture that Nikola Tesla developed.

Always look around, see good things which others are doing, learn from them and get inspired by what they are doing. Again always look around you, see bad things which you don't like, which others are doing every day, learn from their mistakes, because you don't have to waste your time doing the very same mistakes which they are doing. You don't want to be that kind of a person, you should take it easy, take life as your classroom and learn every day.

43

Chapte r 8

Excel what you do

1. The power of imagination

"Pure imagination has no boundaries or constraints. It's free like the wind"

-Beat you goals- David Molden & Denise Parker

Imagination is like a river it flows , the mind's ability to imagine the future is extremely powerful. You can imagine many things, if you allow it to be free from knowledge. Imagination is not an analytical process; it has no borders, conditions, presumption, restrictions, time limits or evaluation criteria.

In my life at some point I use to imagine myself as an author, writing books to motivate people, guiding and give clues in daily life. It was a good feeling, seeing myself shaping how societies think and functions. I had no clue on how to do it by the time, but being curious helps me to re-search and read different books by different authors, just to learn and under-stand the industry before I step in.

Start from imagining myself as a writer, combining with the knowledge that I acquired of how to be a writer, and now, here I am sitting behind my computer writing one of the books which I use to imagine myself writing.

44

I really agree with David molden and Denise parker- Beat your goals, when they say, "The mixture of imagination and knowledge together in the same thinking process and actions, can be a very dangerous cocktail".

In whatever you do, I mean everything you do; don't ever stop imagining yourself doing more. It 's a good thing to imagine and never be satisfied with the way you have always done something, because they may be many more ways available. Just keep on trying, you start from imagining and act, you will end up doing what you use to imagine yourself doing

2. The power of confidence

Confidence is a very precious commodity, those who posses it find it easier to learn new skills, adapt to change, to make new friends, relate to any situations, take challenges on doing something new and achieve what they want in life. Nothing great was ever achieved on planet earth, by the person without a confidence of achieving what he or she is doing.

Increasing confidence is a practical guide to taking charge of your life, because with confidence, life is simply far more enjoyable.

Whether you are writing a book, an interview, meeting, singing, performing, presenting etc., you need to be confident. Confidence is a major asset, which a person should have in life. It helps you deal with uncertainty in your life and you see challenges as opportunity. Confidence gives you courage to tackle challenges, because by dealing with challenges you learn a lot, which is more important than success or failure. It helps in a person's capacity to enjoy life's ups and cope with its downs.

45

People without confidence find it difficult to handle simple situations, deal with problems, to enjoy life to the fullest, because they are always worried about something instead of planning for the future and they also find it difficult to do what they wish to do or to do what they plan to do. If you are confident you feel valued, you feel more in control and you also believe in yourself.

Be confident, because when you are confident, others are likely to entrust you with new challenges, difficult problems to solve and task that require strong leadership and you will also attract more opportunities in everyday life. When you have confidence, you believe that you are more self-determining, that you can influence others, and make things happen. It also helps you form nourishing relationships that are maturely beneficial. The greater the confident levels, the better equipped you are to deal with life's adversities and the more resilient you are.

3. The power of focus

"You cannot excel what you do without focusing, but you can focus and excel at what you do"

People place trust in and are influenced by those they see as being reliable and stay focus on what they do. By focusing on what you do, your talent, people are going to get inspired by what you do, because they will see you as a role model, someone who knows what he is doing. Without focusing on what you are doing, you can't achieve anything or you can't become who you wanted yourself to be.

One day I was watching TV, when South African rugby team was playing against England on a world cup final in France, the year 2007. Before the game I heard Jake white former coach of South African rugby saying, "it's not goi ng to be an easy game, England is a good team, is not an easy

46

team to beat, they are very good in playing rugby, but what we are going to do, we are going to play focusing on winning the game. All players were busy the whole week preparing for this game, so the only thing which we are going to do is to focus only on winning the game". And again after the game, I heard him sayin g, "it was not a simple game, England were playing very good rugby, they were supposed to beat us, but only because we were focusing on winning the game, we won. Our players were very much focused and they have done it"

I said to myself, wow they have won the world cup final, only because they were playing against England focusing on winning. That's when I start to see the power of focus; I start to believe that by focusing anything is simple. There is no other way that you can drive a car and arrive where you are going safe, without focusing on the road, because if you don't focus on the road you are going to cause accidents.

Focus is very important in life. I have seen many people losing focus on what they do. I remember MG general supermarket, one of the biggest supermarket in our village of the time. I was still young by the time, but I have seen it when the owner of MG supermarket start to lose focus, it was very simple for him to manage his supermarket and that's what he use to do, because the whole village use to buy everything in that supermarket. He was the biggest supplier. After some few years, he start to use his status in a wrong way, dating young people and he was a family man, a role model to young boys in the village, he was very focused on the business but after start-ing these dating thing, he start to lose focus on his business, he forgot that the business was the only way he use to generate money. He forgot to focus on growing the business and start to focus on spending money with those beautiful young girls of the village. He impregnated two girls in the village and after some few months the business started to collapse, be-cause the owner

47

was no longer focused on it, he was focusing on solving his problems, which he created himself by forgetting that he is a family man and a business man. He used the money for the business to solve his problems and to impress ladies, instead of using it to grow the business. His bakkie's were sold and after a couple of months he was a pedestrian and when people were still surprised on what's happening, the supermarket got closed until further notice.

"If you focus on what you do best, you are guaranteed to succeed in life"

Focus is the most important thing when doing what you do, why? Because you cannot excel what you do without focusing, but you can focus and excel at what you do. In whatever you do, it doesn't matter what it is, don't ever lose focus, because everything will fall apart, always stay focus. Here in South Africa there are many things which cause talented people to lose focus. I have seen many people, soccer players, radio DJs, artists, athletes' etc., loosing focus on what they do, because of drugs and alcohol. So in whatever you do, you must stay focus in order to excel at what you do.

Chapter 9

Help others as well

"Kindness has the ability to manifest more of itself, be kind always; you will love the way it makes you feel"

Release others expectations; if you focus on what others expect of you, you will continue to act on and attract more what they desire for you. Always choose to be kind! Whatever you are trying to achieve in life will usually require the assistance of others. When you perform act of kindness on others they will feel uplifted, your influence will be felt and others will draw to you. By always practicing kindness you will find that the universe will support you in ways you could never have predicted.

The secret of world peace, for, we cannot depend on countries or government, to do it as entities, for we are all, each of us as individuals, the entities that make up those countries and governments. Let peace begin with us as individuals. Kindness is very powerful and touching, many times I have felt emotional and depressed, but end up feeling very good by the smallest act of kindness of others. By just giving someone who is asking for money or food in a street you will feel very good and you will also be proud of yourself; try it always, it's amazing.

We cannot have the relationship with god and then treat others adversely. Let kindness become epidemic; when one actively expresses random acts of kindness it's only an extension of god. Just imagine Doctors and Nurses, kindness

49

towards others is what they do each an everyday of their lives; saving people's life and not expecting anything in return. Compassion is the way of changing this world, one person at a time; be patient and willing to help others, always keep love and light in your heart for all others no matter what they may have done, but in your life brings you a gift or a lesson.

1. Be a leader

"You can have everything in life you want if you will just help enough other people to get what they want" – Zig Zigler

There will never be a better time than now to take control of your thoughts. Our dominant thoughts drive our actions, which lead to results and failure is only postponed success as long as courage coaches ambition. The habit of persistence is the habit of victory. Be a patient leader of your life and others as well.

The late former South African first black president Nelson Mandela said " The greatest glory in living lies not in ever falling, but in rising every time you fall." He did a lot of things for South Africa; by being patient and believing in other people as well; he lead from the back and let others believe they are in front. He believed in others as well, he knew that if he lead others well, showed them a way and give them courage everything is going to be possible. He turned the table and end up by saying, "It's always seems impossible until it's done".

Be content to stand in the light and let the shadow fall where it will; it is courage that make anything possible, live bravely and present a brave front to adversity, be an example to other, be an inspiration to the young ones.

50

"The greatest block to a person's de velopment is his having to take on a way of life which is not rooted in his own powers." –R May

2. Do your purpose

Cast of characters:

I can't is a quitter,
I don 't know is lazy,
I wish I could is a wisher,
I might is waking up,
I will try is on his feet,
I can is on his way,
I will is at work,
I did is now the boss

-Earl Cassel

Each day can be one of triumph if you keep up your interests in things around you. Most people give up just when they are about to achieve success, they give up and quit what they are doing at the last minute of the game. It take time to succeed because success is merely the natural reward of taking time to do anything well, giving yourself time to plan and work hard on what you want to achieve in life. Success seems to be connected with action, successful people keep moving; even though they make mistakes just like any other person, but they don't quit.

Never underestimate yourself, never look down on yourself, and never discourage you rself. Don't ask yourself what the world needs, ask yourself what makes you come alive and what purpose are you living for; and after go out there do youpurpose, because what the world need is people who live for their purpose.

51

"You come into th e world with nothing, and the purpose of your life is to make something out of nothing."

-Henry Mencken

3. Inspire others

"Make happy those who are near and those who are far will come"
-Chinese Proverb

The things that you do should be things that you love, when you do something that you love, you have enough courage and passion to achieve all your goals, when you achieve all your goals you become successful and when become successful you inspire others; after being inspired by your success, they work hard to become successful just like you and after all the world will become a better place.

Every event is subjective, not what it means that matters, but what it means to you and others as well. You are meant to think before you speak, and every act should be a spiritual one involving your total being which is soul, mind and body; done for the doing of given for the sake of giving, worked for the sake of working and not for the sake of what you get from it. Look around you and see what others are doing, Mark Zuckerberg the founder of the giant social media which everyone is using today all over the world " Facebook", he gave himself time to create something which the whole world is benefiting today. As soon as you allow where you are to be all right, you will able to get where you want to be much faster than you thought.

Larry Page and Sergey Brin came up with "Google", which is the most reliable source of any information which a person can look for and get it faster, it is very useful to people all over the world, everyone need it. They didn't do it for

52

themselves only, but for the world as a whole. If you are serious about conscious creating the life you love, you will want to sign up for one and then support, guidance and techniques will all deliver itself to you. Everything around you was a thought in someone's mind before it existence in your reality. Consciously creating your reality means you can take one hundred percent responsibility for all areas of your life and your world, and that means you can change your wold substantively.

"Since you are like no other being created since the beginning of the time, you are incomparable."

-Brenda Ueland

53

Chapter 10

It is all up to you

"If you forget you have to struggle for improvement, you go backward." – Geoffrey Hickson

Now everything is all about you, you need to decide how you handle your future; the African proverb says: "When there is no enemy within, the enemies outside can't hurt you". Remember, in life every statement you make about yourself, to your friend, family, colleagues and even to yourself, become the truth. You are the one who is in control of everything, you project energy every moment for everything you do and only you can create for yourself what you want.

So I believe in you, I know you can do it because nothing can stop you. So let's talk about your dream, if it's really that important to you, to create the reality you say you prefer, you will do what it takes, you will do anything, you will be hungry to create a vibration of passion within you all the time; if the answer within yourself to that is "yes", it means that you have any permission slip or a tool available to you, you will use it as often as you can and achieve everything.

A belief is nothing more than a chronic pattern of thought, you have the ability, if you try a little bit to begin a new pattern, to achieve a different vibration, to change a point of vibration, and to change the point of attraction. As you begin to positively focus, getting to feel so good about so many subjects, you will begin to feel the power that creates world flowing through you.

Barbara De Angelis said, "Passion acts like a magnet that attracts us to its source; we are drawn to people who radiate with passion, who live with passion, who breathe with passion. Your passion is your true power, the more you

54

discover and express your passion for life, the more irresistible you will become to others."

1. Positive focus

"I don't believe you have to be better than everybody else, I believe you have to be better than you ever thought you could be." -Ken Venturi

Positivity is gratitude and appreciation for where you were, where you are, and where you are going. Being outrageously happy is a great future to focus on and happy now is what creates future happiness. Life can be very easy to manage and very simple to understand; one good reason so few of us achieve what we truly want is that we never direct our focus; we never concentrate our power. Most people dabble their way through life, never deciding to master anything in particular; but if we put our positive focus through life, concentrate our power on what we want, we can all end up achieving our goals.

Your quality of life is shaped and determined by what you feed inside your subconscious mind. If you once impress your subconscious mind and start to own your dream with your mind's eye then subconscious mind will drive you on the highway of life and success breaking all flood gates of impossibilities, and you will be driven by the subconscious mind with full momentum, enthusiasm, massive passionate action, strong self-belief, strong faith on lord and strong courage on success. With positive focus you will never be ordinary like others who tend to live their fears instead of living their dreams.

"It has been my observation that most people get ahead during the time that others waste" –Henry Ford

55

We have seen it many times in many things like: sports, acting, businesses etc. I grew up watching Denzel Washington movies, knowing that he is the best actor who even wins an Oscar, but I was surprised one day when I was watching his interview on TV in a live show; when he was asked how he did it, being the best actor. And when he answered, he put it in a simple way: "I don't take myself serious, I take what I do very serious because it's what makes who I am."

One day I was sitting with my cousin watching some music awards and DJ Khaled, the much known hip hop producer and beats creator won an award, and he was given chance to speak in front of everyone and he didn't say much, he just went to the stage and said: "We work hard ma n, we are the best; thank you." My cousin was laughing because he was expecting to hear a speech from DJ Khaled, just like what others were doing, I was also laughing but not because I was expecting to hear a well prepared speech from him, but because of his honesty. I knew he was telling the truth because being a DJ and Producer takes a lot of efforts, with a lot of positive focus.

Lewis Hamilton proved that he is the best when he breaks Michael Schumacher's record of 91 race wins on formula one in Portuguese GP 2020. That's what we call positive focus, working hard on what you do, to be the best.

"If you limit your actions in life to things that nobody can possibly find fault with, you will not do much." –Charles Dodgson

56

2. Successes

"Life is a grindstone, whether it grinds a man down or polishes him up depends on the stuff he's made of."

-Josh Billings

Success is living up to your potential, that 's all. Wake up with a smile and go after life, live it, enjoy it, taste it, smell it and feel it. Success is almost totally dependent upon drive and persistence. The extra energy required to make another effort or try another approach is the secret of winning.

Let me tell you the secret that has led me to my goal, my strength lays solely in my tenacity. I am not the smartest or the most talented person in the world, but I succeeded because I keep going, going and going. I don 't give up and I will never give up in my life; I believe that life can be pulled by goals just as surely as it can be pushed by drives. And character cannot be developed in ease and quite, only through experience of trial and suffering, the soul can be strengthened, vision cleared, ambition inspired and success achieved.

A man can succeed at almost anything for which he has unlimited enthusiasm, yes, but the problem with most people is that they think of their goals as impossible and that's where failing begins. If you are insecure, guess what? The rest of the world is too. Do not overestimate the competition and underestimate yourself, because you are better than you think you are. Most people gain wisdom more readily through their failure than through their successes. They always think of failure as the antithesis of success, but isn't. Success often lies just on the other side of failure.

57

Speak in such a way that others love to listen to you and listen in such a way that others love to speak to you, that's what successful people do. Be strong but not rude; be kind but not weak; be bold but not a bully; be humble but not timid, and be proud but not arrogant, that's how successful people live.

"We don't pay the price for success; we pay the price for failure. We enjoy the benefits of success." –Zig Ziglar

58

Chapter 11

Manage Ups and Downs Situations

In life we come across the ups and downs situations in whatever that we are doing, it might be in your career, love, business, and even in every day's life that we are living. No one can stand in front of people and tell them his/her life is perfect in such a way that he/she doesn't face any challenges in everyday of their life.

No matter your rich or poor you will face some ups and downs situations in your life. It depends on how you handle those situations, because people handle them in a different way.

"Nobody can go back and start a new beginning but anyone can start today and make a new ending"

-Maria Robinson

1. Ups situation

These is the kind of situations where everything will be happening the way you have been always wanted in your life. What's sad about this situation is that most people get over excited about it and forget where they are coming from, the entire struggle they have been through, and tend to ruin everything they have achieved. I have seen a lot people who have manage to make it up for there, and get over excited about it and at the end they lose focus in everything and start doing things which will put them back to square one where they started and all that happen because of drinking too much, doing of drugs, and a lot of things which are not related to what they are do for living.

59

You can achieve all your goals and become successful, but you don't have to forget where you come from and where you are going. In the world of success limiting yourself in most of unwanted situations, hobbies or commitments, is very important. You need to make sure, by all means that you don't get distracted up there where you are, because you have been working so hard to be there, and you know you don't want to lose the opportunity that you are having now, which you have worked so hard to get, which makes you the most excited person, and which make others to wish to be like you. Consider yourself very luck, and be thankful that you are a winner, an achiever and a role model to others.

Success is never a destination, it is a journey, just because you are up there doesn't mean you need to feel that you have arrived and you have everything that you always wanted and start to relax, no, that's the biggest mistake you can do. Tell yourself you no longer allow the negative things in your life to spoil all the good things you have, things that you have worked for, you choose to be happy and you are still in a mission to achieve more. Continue working hard, you start it and you can still finish it, yes, you have to.

Your achievement should be what you love, and you must place your focus on what you love rather than what you hate. Think, speak, and act from love. Remember that contrast serves a purpose as it allow you to feel what you don't want and refocus on what you do want.

"Life pays for performance; you get out of it what you pay forward" –Scottie Somers

60

2. Down Situations

In this situation things will never seems to be going according to your plan, every living individual face a situations like this in his/her life; but that doesn't mean that you have to give up in everything that you are doing, this is the situation which need a person to be strong enough to face, because this is the kind of situation which can bring a person down. It require a person to be strong enough to face, giving up is not a solution for someone who want to achieve something. I have seen a lot of business closing down, a lot of people quitting what they are doing, and a lot of people committing suicide because of the down situation; people get traumatised or depressed of this situation and think that nothing will ever work out.

You need to be strong enough to face this kind of situation, just know that progress is impossible without change, and those who cannot change their mind cannot change anything. You don't need more great opportunities or more money to deal with this kind of situation, but all you need is more strength and courage to be able to adapt with the situation, in order to be able to deal with it. The majority of men meet with failure because of their lack of persistence in creating new plans to deal with the down situation they face in life.

"There is no reason to ever quit, unless of course, you had no plans to ever succeed" –Doug Firebaugh

Getting an idea should be like sitting down on a pin; it should make you jump up and do something, to fuel up your action to achieve your goal, which you are aiming to achieve. The moment one definitely commits oneself, and then providence moves too; all sorts of things occur to help that would never otherwise have occurred.

61

You must understand that difficulties, mistakes and setbacks are an inevitable part of life, career, and business. Don't allow them to knock you off your feet, you must be tough, be focused, there are a lot of downs but you can ride them out if you are strong and well prepared enough to see yourself back up of the ladder where you want to see yourself. You must keep your momentum, because without your momentum everything; I mean ideas, plans, goals, and courage go nowhere. You must look at the problem's solution and not the problem itself; learn to focus on what will give results.

"This is the world of action, and not for moping and droning in." –Charles Dickens

If you willing to do only what's easy, life will be hard ; but if you are willing to do what's hard, life will be very easy for you. One thing you should know, which is very important is that, formal education will make you a living; and on the other side, self-education will make you a fortune. Always be in a mission of learning new things every day, learn to handle every situation. In life the major value is not what you get, but what you become is the major value, and success is not to be pursued; but to be attracted by the person you become.

A positive attitude may not solve every problem, but it makes solving problem a more pleasant experience. You need to have positive attitude always when you face any situation and forget all things which are not important; it must be your mistakes or failures happened to you before, and start thinking about what you are going to do next to get out of the down situation and get back up were you where before. Your ability can put you back to the top, but it also takes character to keep you there; make sure you don't repeat the same mistake again, and avoid all things which can put you back to the situation which you don't want to be on.

Cha pter 12

Self-discipline, and live large

"Life is like riding a bicycle, to keep you r balance, you must keep moving."
–Albeit Einstein

You are given the gift of gods; you create your reality according to your beliefs, yours is the creative energy that makes your world; there are no limitations to the self except those you believe in. success comes in can and failure in can'ts; never use the word I can't, you must be positive enough to always use words like, I can, I will, and I am going to.

It 's not the events of our lives that shape us, but our beliefs as to what those events means to us. To many people it is easy to sit up, take notice and what is very difficult to them is getting up and taking action; so unlike them you are not scared to act in whatever that you want to do, and you are strong enough in such a way that if you fell down yesterday, you will stand up today and continue doing what you are supposed to be doing. Just know that your mind work for you and not someone else, the goal you have set is yours to achieve and not someone else.

Having self-discipline, to be able to control yourself, guide yourself, motivate yourself, advice yourself, and being the leader of your own journey, is what I expect from you. You are a yardstick of quality; other people 's minds are not used to an environment where excellence is expected and you are living in a free world where everything is possible. Never lead yourself in a wrong direction, you are in a right track, so have self-discipline and live large, the life you always wanted. Work hard and smile when you see the results of your hard work, enjoy and do more.

63

Self-discipline

"It is wise to direct your anger towards problems, not people; to focus energies on answers, not excuses." -William A. Ward

Always be self-discipline, how you live your life; how you do what you do; how you talk to other people, how you handle your situations- family, business, love, work etc. whatever your grade or position, no matter how successful you are; know how and when to speak and also when to remain silent. Look for the meaning of life within yourself, if you want to find deeper meaning in your life; you can't find it in the opinions or the beliefs that have been handed to you; you have to go that place and find it within yourself.

Life is not about waiting for the storm to pass, it is about learning to dance in the rain. You must learn to manage everything in your life, don't ever take anything for granted, everything must be meaningful to you, weather good or bad you must learn from it. In this life we must all suffer one of these three things: the pain of discipline or the pain of regret or the pain of disappointment. Be discipline enough not to suffer the pain of regret, try all your best not to do things that you will end up regretting. Also live your life avoiding disappointment, don't live your life expecting too much from people, just do it yourself. How you see your future is much more important than what happened in your past. At the end of the life, what really matters is not what we bought but what we built; not what we got but what we shared, not our competence but our character; and not our success, but our significance; live a life that matters.

The greatest secret for eliminating the inferiority complex is to fill your mind to overflow with faith. If you expect the worst you will get the worst and if you expect the best you will get the best.

64

Live large

"Be happy in the moment, that's enough. Each moment is all we need, not more." – Mother Teresa

Living your dream is nobody's business but your own. So put your back on it, lean forward and walk towards it because it is not going to come chasing you down anytime soon. In order to manifest, to take part in the process of co-creating your life and attracting to yourself the objects of your heart desires, you must know that you are worthy of receiving. Manifesting involves using the power of your inner world to craft a fuller relationship with life.

You have to put in many tiny efforts that nobody sees or appreciates before you achieve anything worthwhile. You need to be always happy in whatever things you do, and trust is like the air we breathe, when trust is present, no one notices, but when there is no trust anyone notice. If you learn to appreciate more of what you already have, you will find yourself having more to appreciate in your life

"A man 's character will make himself worthy of any position he is given" –Mahatma Gandhi

Live your dream, the life you always wanted to live. If your actions inspire others to dream more, learn more, do more, and become more, that's means you are a leader. Learning is a change in behaviour, you haven't learned a thing until you can take action and use it. The beautiful thing about learning is that nobody can take it away from you, and please don't ever let your learning lead to knowledge only; also let your learning lead to action.

65

Take good care of everything you have achieve, enjoy the results of your hard work, never mind spoiling yourself but don't overdo it. Make sure that whatever you do you do it because is necessary to be done by you, is your life be the best you can be. Always be happy because you have something to be happy about, your achievement isn't it that great, yes, it the best thing and it must be something that you live to protect, it supposed to be your best priority.

You can spend your life any way you want to, be innovative. Innovative people are creative, they are flexible and adaptable. Through change we each have the opportunity to reach our potential. The type of leader who is needed in this century must be secure enough to have principle based leadership as their anchor. Just do your part and leave everything to God.

"Integrity is doing what you said you will do, when you said you will do it, and how you said you would do it"

-Byrd Baggett

66

Acknowledgements

I notice roles which others play in my life; they are friends who are there to build you. We need more reassurance, more help, more support and more than our share of love. I thank Tshimangadzo Gwalidi for his faith in the book reflected by his words of encouragement, critic and support. I thank Ntokozo Ndukula, my friend who labored to design the book. He showed loyalty everyday; his tireless and selfless work has not gone unnoticed.

67

About the Author

Khodani Emmanuel Maudu grew up in Ngudza village, about seven kilometres out of Thohoyandou town, in Limpopo province. He holds a bachelor's degree in Media Studies from the University of Limpopo. Emmanuel has been interested in writing for a long time. For him words are forever existing, writer's shape how societies think and function. For purpose he writes and wants to change the world. In his mission to inspire people to be their best he encourages anyone to use their talents. With a passion of helping people to fulfil their true potential and transform the importance they have in life and in whatever they do. He wants everyone to be free to use their talent, he grew up seeing many talented people, who've fail to use their talent, only because they where afraid, some didn't believe in themselves, they didn't have courage and now he believe it's time for you to change, time for you to discover the nature of your own particular genius, because everyone is talented.

www.ingramcontent.com/pod-product-compliance
Lightning Source LLC
LaVergne TN
LVHW051429080426
835508LV00022B/3314